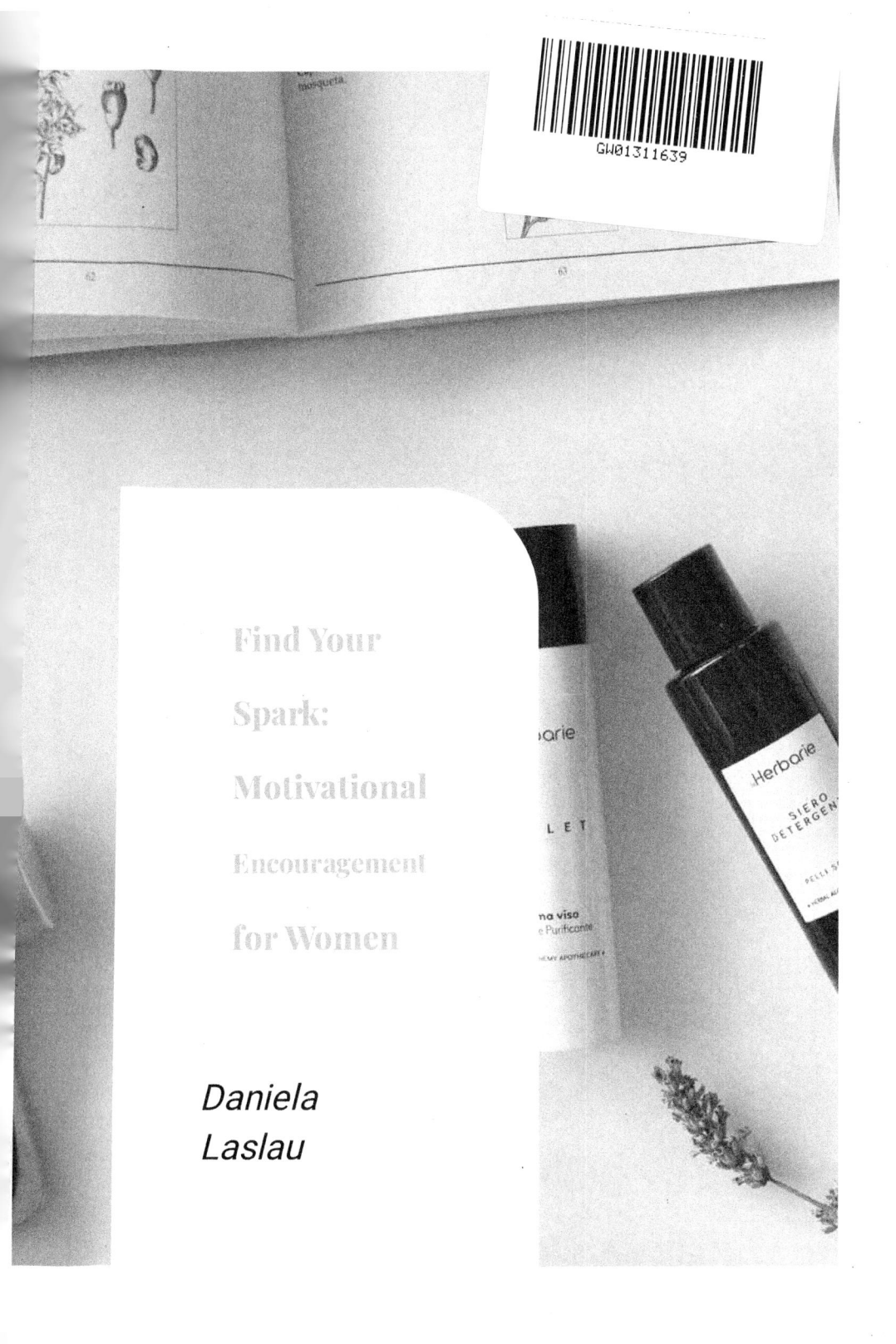

Find Your Spark: Motivational Encouragement for Women

Daniela Laslau

Table of Content :

Find Your Spark: Motivational Encouragement for Women

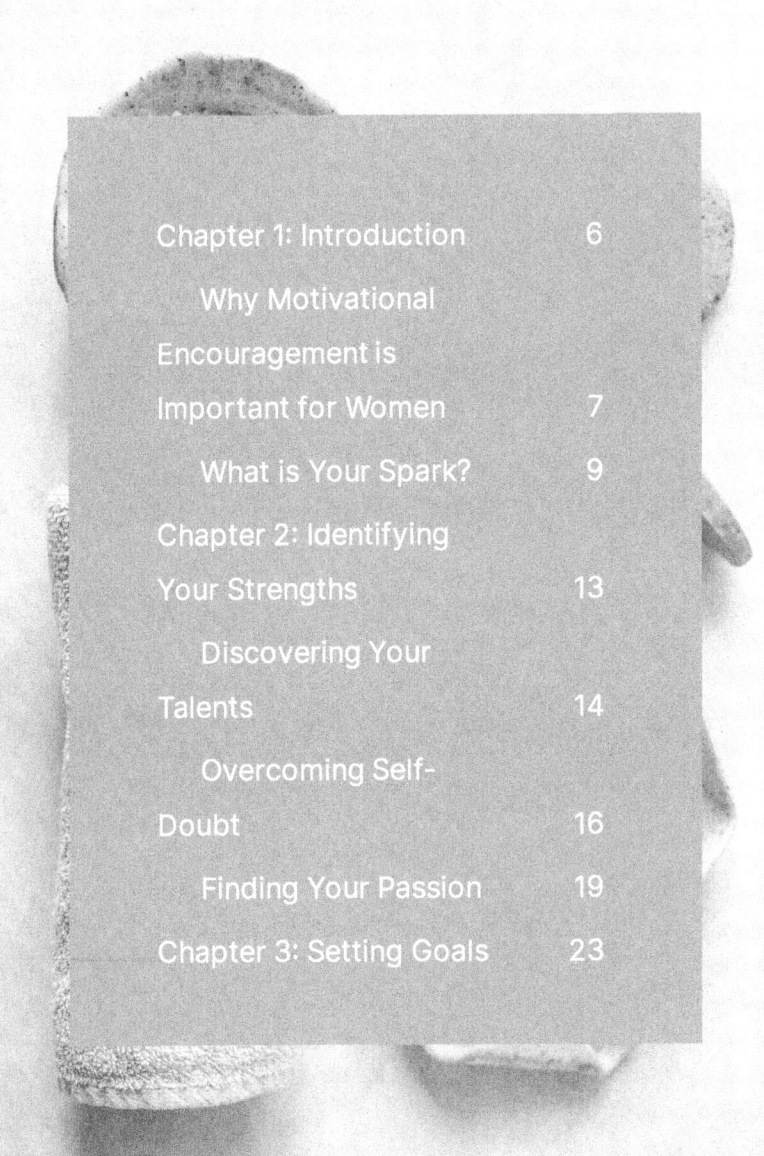

Find Your Spark: Motivational Encouragement for Women

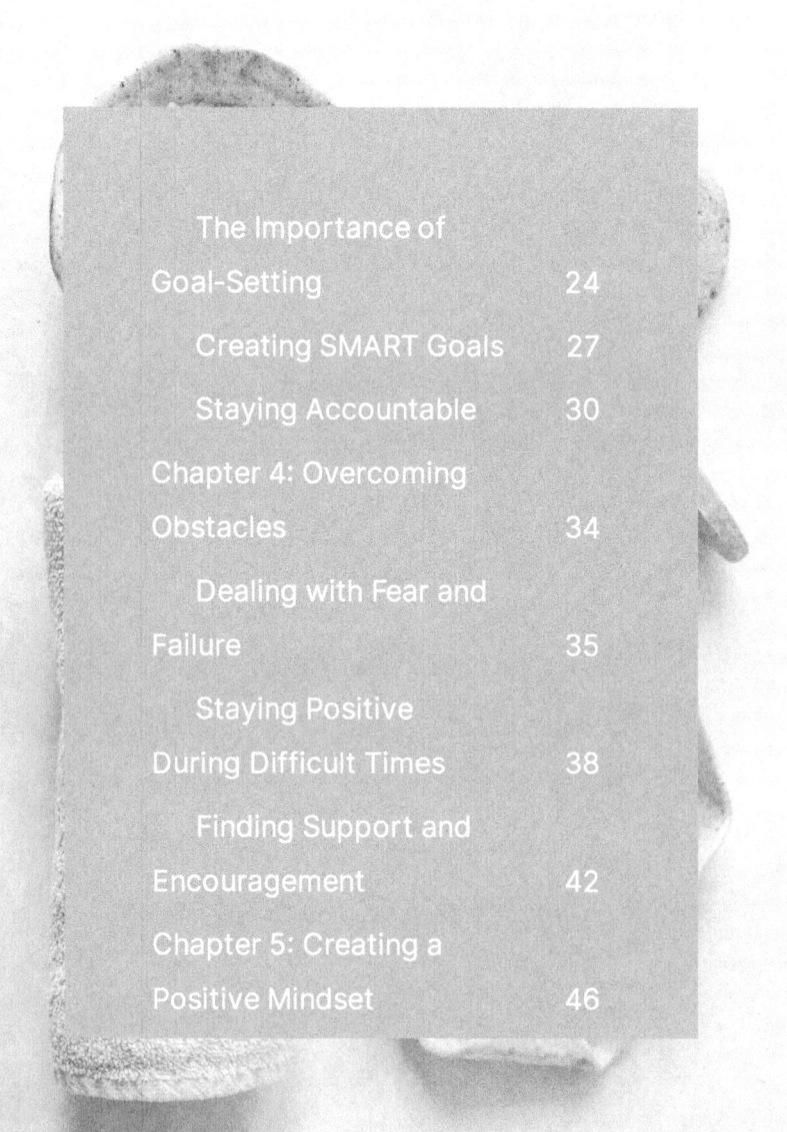

Find Your Spark: Motivational Encouragement for Women

Find Your Spark: Motivational Encouragement for Women

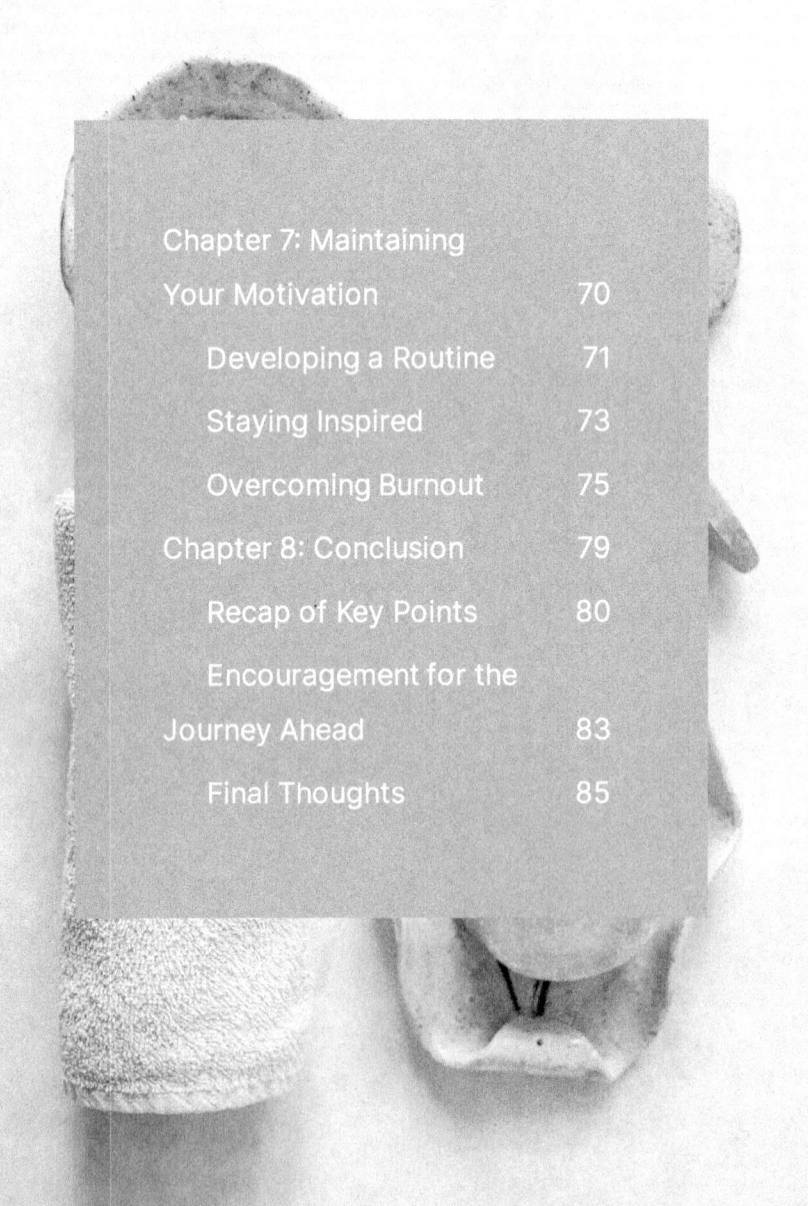

Find Your Spark: Motivational Encouragement for
Women

01

Chapter 1: Introduction

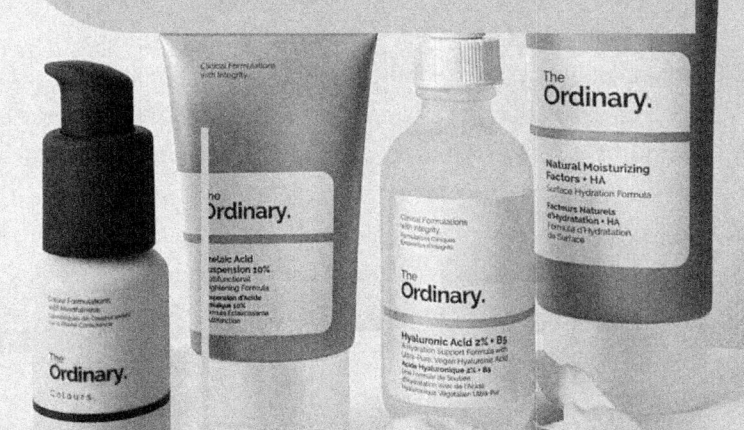

Find Your Spark: Motivational Encouragement for Women

Why Motivational Encouragement is Important for Women

and "personal development."

Motivational encouragement is important for women because it can help women to overcome the challenges they face in their personal and professional lives. Women often have to juggle multiple responsibilities, such as caring for children, managing a household, and pursuing a career. This can be overwhelming, and women may feel like they are not doing any of these tasks well. This is where motivational encouragement comes in.

Motivational encouragement can help women to see the positive aspects of their lives and to focus on their strengths. It can help them to overcome self-doubt and to believe in themselves. When women feel motivated and encouraged, they are more likely to take risks and to pursue their goals. They are also more likely to bounce back from setbacks and to persevere in the face of challenges.

Motivational encouragement can also help women to connect with others who share their goals and aspirations. Women can form support networks and find mentors who can offer guidance and advice. These networks can be invaluable in helping women to achieve their goals and to overcome obstacles.

In addition, motivational encouragement can help women to develop a positive mindset. Women who are optimistic and hopeful are more likely to be successful in their personal and professional lives. They are also more likely to be happy and fulfilled.

By focusing on the positive aspects of their lives and by setting achievable goals, women can develop a sense of purpose and direction.

In conclusion, motivational encouragement is important for women because it can help them to overcome the challenges they face and to achieve their goals. By focusing on their strengths, connecting with others, and developing a positive mindset, women can find their spark and live a fulfilling life. This book, "Find Your Spark: Motivational Encouragement for Women," provides practical advice and inspiration for women who want to find their spark and achieve their dreams.

What is Your Spark?

Find Your Spark: Motivational Encouragement for Women

and "self-help".

What is Your Spark?

As women, we often find ourselves searching for our purpose in life. We try different things, take up new hobbies, and explore different paths, all in the hopes of finding something that truly ignites us. But what if I told you that your spark was already inside of you, waiting to be discovered?

Your spark is your passion—the thing that sets your soul on fire. It's the thing that makes you feel alive—the thing that you could do for hours on end without ever getting bored. It's the thing that you were put on this earth to do.

Find Your Spark: Motivational Encouragement for Women

But how do you find your spark? It starts with self-exploration. You need to take the time to get to know yourself on a deeper level. What makes you happy? What are your strengths? What are your values? What are your goals? These are all important questions to ask yourself.

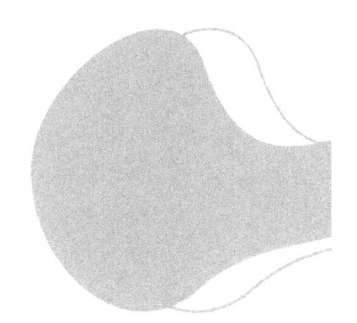

Once you have a better understanding of who you are, it's time to start trying new things. Take up a new hobby, try a new sport, or sign up for a class. You never know what you might discover.

But don't just try things for the sake of trying them. Pay attention to how they make you feel. Do you feel energised? Excited? Happy? If so, you might be onto something.

It's also important to remember that your spark doesn't have to be something grandiose or world-changing. It could be something as simple as baking, gardening, or writing. The important thing is that it brings you joy.

Once you've found your spark, it's important to nurture it. Make time for it in your life. Surround yourself with people who support and encourage you. And don't be afraid to share it with the world.

Remember, your spark is what sets you apart from everyone else. It's what makes you unique. Embrace it and let it light up your life.

O2

Chapter 2: Identifying Your Strengths

Find Your Spark: Motivational Encouragement for Women

Discovering Your Talents

and "self-improvement"

Discovering Your Talents

Do you ever feel like you're not living up to your full potential? Like there's something more out there for you, but you're not sure what it is? It's a common feeling, especially for women who have been taught to put others first and prioritize their responsibilities over their own passions.

The key to unlocking your full potential is discovering your talents. Talents are those unique abilities and skills that come naturally to you. They're things that you enjoy doing and that make you feel fulfilled. When you're using your talents, you're in a state of flow, where time seems to stand still and you're completely absorbed in what you're doing.

The first step in discovering your talents is to pay attention to what comes naturally to you. What are the things that you're good at without even trying? What do people compliment you on? What do you enjoy doing in your free time? These are all clues to your natural talents.

Another way to discover your talents is to try new things. Take a class in something that interests you, whether it's painting, cooking, or learning a new language. Volunteer for a project at work that's outside of your usual job duties. Join a club or group that aligns with your interests. Trying new things will help you discover hidden talents that you might not have realized you had.

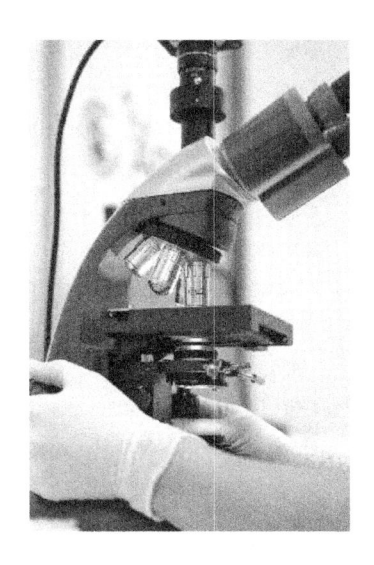

Once you've identified your talents, it's important to nurture them. Practice and develop your skills, whether it's through formal education, mentorship, or self-study. Surround yourself with people who support and encourage you, and seek out opportunities to use your talents in meaningful ways.

Discovering your talents is not only important for your personal fulfillment, but it can also have a positive impact on your career and relationships. When you're using your talents, you're more likely to be successful and fulfilled in your work, and you'll have more to offer in your relationships.

So take the time to discover your talents and nurture them. You never know where they might lead you.

Overcoming Self-Doubt

and "self-improvement". Overcoming Self-Doubt

Find Your Spark: Motivational Encouragement for Women

Self-doubt is a common obstacle that many women face when pursuing their dreams and goals. It can be paralyzing and prevent us from taking the necessary steps to achieve our full potential. However, it is important to remember that self-doubt is a normal part of the journey towards success. The key is to overcome it and not let it control our lives. The first step in overcoming self-doubt is to acknowledge it. Recognize when those negative thoughts start creeping in and try to identify the root cause of them. Is it fear of failure? Lack of confidence? Once you have a better understanding of where the self-doubt is coming from, you can start to address it head-on.

One effective way to overcome self-doubt is to practice self-compassion. Treat yourself with the same kindness and understanding that you would offer to a friend who is struggling. It is important to remind yourself that it is okay to make mistakes and that failure is a natural part of the learning process.

Another helpful technique is to focus on your strengths and accomplishments. Make a list of your achievements, both big and small, and remind yourself of them regularly. This will help boost your confidence and remind you of your capabilities. Surrounding yourself with positive and supportive people can also be beneficial in overcoming self-doubt. Seek out friends, family, or even a mentor who believe in you and can provide encouragement and motivation when you need it most.

Fi... ...or
Women

Lastly, it is important to take action and face your fears. Often, self-doubt can stem from a fear of the unknown or a fear of failure. But the only way to truly overcome these fears is to confront them and take action towards your goals. Start with small steps and build momentum as you go.

Remember, self-doubt is a normal part of the journey towards success. But with a little self-compassion, focus on your strengths, a supportive network, and taking action, you can overcome it and achieve your full potential.

Finding Your Passion

and "self-improvement."
Finding Your Passion

As women, it's easy to get caught up in our daily routines and forget about the things that truly light us up inside. We may have jobs or responsibilities that we feel obligated to fulfill, but it's important to remember that we're not living our fullest lives if we're not pursuing our passions.

So how do you find your passion? It's not always an easy question to answer, but here are a few tips to help you get started:

1. Think back to your childhood. What did you love to do when you were young? Did you have any hobbies or interests that you've since abandoned? Revisiting these pastimes could help you rediscover a passion you've been missing.

2. Consider your strengths. What are you good at? What do your friends and family come to you for help with? Your passions are often related to your natural talents.

3. Try new things. You may have a hidden passion for something you've never even tried before. Sign up for a class or workshop in an area that interests you and see how it feels.

4. Pay attention to what excites you. When you're scrolling through social media or reading a magazine, take note of the things that catch your eye. What topics make you want to learn more?

Once you've identified your passion, it's important to make time for it in your life. This may mean rearranging your schedule or cutting back on other commitments, but the fulfillment you'll get from pursuing your passion will be worth it. Remember, it's never too late to find your passion. Whether you're in your 20s or your 60s, there's always time to explore new interests and discover what truly sets your soul on fire. Don't be afraid to take risks and try new things – you never know where your passion may lead you.

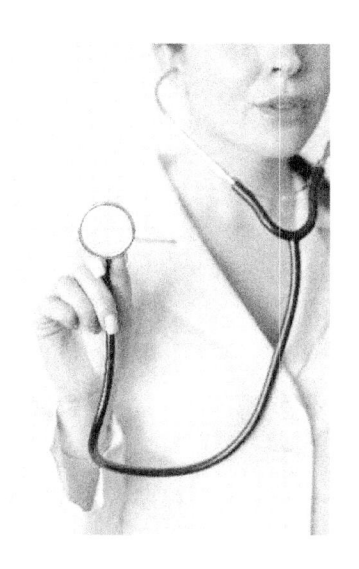

Find Your Spark: Motivational Encouragement for Women

03

Chapter 3: Setting Goals

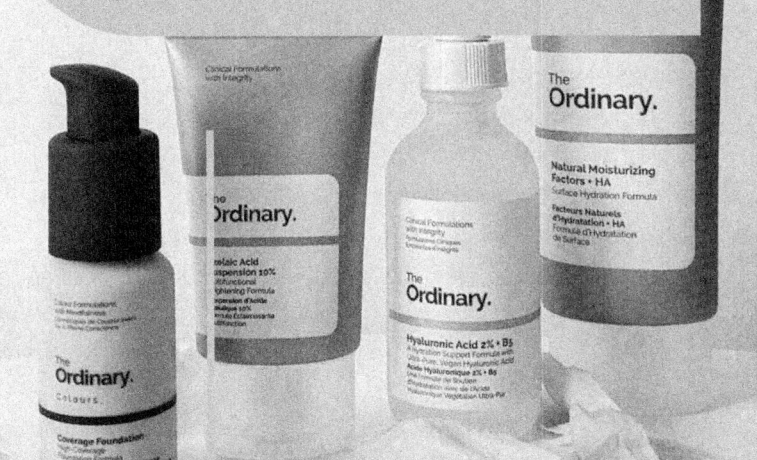

Find Your Spark: Motivational Encouragement for Women

The Importance of Goal-Setting

and "self-improvement".

The Importance of Goal-Setting

Goal-setting is a crucial aspect of personal development and growth. Without a clear sense of direction, it's easy to feel lost and unmotivated. By setting goals, you give yourself a roadmap to follow, which helps you stay focused and driven.

As women, we often have a lot of competing priorities, whether it's work, family, or personal commitments. It can be challenging to prioritize our own goals and dreams amidst these responsibilities. However, neglecting our own needs and aspirations can lead to feelings of dissatisfaction and unfulfillment.

Goal-setting allows us to take control of our lives and make intentional decisions about what we want to achieve. By identifying specific objectives, we can break down larger, more complex goals into manageable steps. This makes the process of reaching our goals feel less daunting and more achievable.

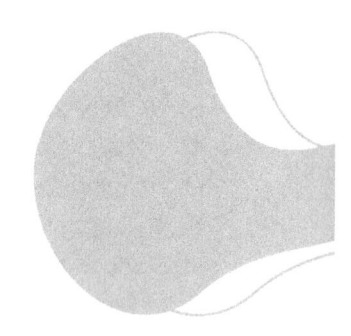

In addition to providing direction and focus, goal-setting also helps us measure our progress. When we have clear benchmarks to aim for, we can track our success and celebrate our achievements along the way. This sense of accomplishment can be a powerful motivator, spurring us on to tackle even bigger challenges.

Of course, setting goals is just the first step. It's essential to follow through on our plans and take action towards our objectives. This requires discipline, determination, and a willingness to overcome obstacles and setbacks along the way.

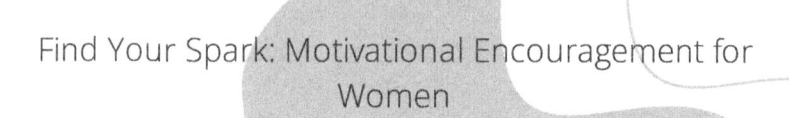

If you're struggling to set goals for yourself, start by reflecting on what's important to you and what you want to achieve. Consider both short-term and long-term goals and be specific about what you hope to accomplish. Write down your goals and break them down into smaller, achievable steps. Then, hold yourself accountable by tracking your progress and adjusting your approach as needed.

By setting goals and pursuing them with intention and determination, you can unlock your full potential and achieve the success and fulfillment you deserve. So, take the time to identify your goals and start taking action towards achieving them today.

Creating SMART Goals

and "self-improvement".

Creating SMART Goals

Setting goals is an essential part of achieving success in any area of life. However, not all goals are created equal. Many women set goals that are vague, unrealistic, or unattainable, leading to frustration and disappointment. To ensure that your goals are effective and achievable, it is essential to create SMART goals.

SMART is an acronym for Specific, Measurable, Achievable, Relevant, and Time-bound. SMART goals help you to focus your efforts, track your progress, and stay motivated. Let's take a closer look at each of these components.

Specific: Your goal should be clear and well-defined. Avoid setting vague goals like "get fit" or "lose weight." Instead, be specific about what you want to achieve. For example, "lose 10 pounds in three months" or "run a 5k in under 30 minutes."

Measurable: Your goal should have a way to measure progress and success. This will help you to track your progress and stay motivated. For example, if your goal is to lose 10 pounds in three months, you can measure your progress by weighing yourself weekly or taking measurements.

Achievable: Your goal should be challenging but attainable. Avoid setting goals that are too easy or too difficult. Consider your current abilities, resources, and time constraints when setting your goal.

Relevant: Your goal should be relevant to your overall life goals and values. It should be something that motivates and inspires you. For example, if your overall goal is to live a healthier lifestyle, losing 10 pounds in three months may be relevant.

Time-bound: Your goal should have a deadline or timeline. This will help you to stay focused and motivated. For example, if your goal is to run a 5k in under 30 minutes, you can set a deadline of three months from now.

In conclusion, setting SMART goals is an effective way to achieve success in any area of life. By creating specific, measurable, achievable, relevant, and time-bound goals, you can focus your efforts, track your progress, and stay motivated.

Remember to celebrate your successes along the way and adjust your goals as needed. With SMART goals, you can find your spark and achieve your dreams.

Staying Accountable

and "self-help".
Staying Accountable

As women, we all have dreams and goals that we aim to achieve. However, sometimes we may lack the motivation or determination to see them through. This is where accountability comes in. Being accountable means taking ownership of your actions and being responsible for the outcomes. It is a crucial element in achieving success. Accountability is not only necessary in our personal lives but also in our professional lives. Whether you are working towards a promotion or starting a new business venture, being accountable can help you stay focused, motivated, and on track towards your goals.

Here are some tips on how to stay accountable:

1. Set Clear Goals

The first step in staying accountable is to set clear goals. Without clear goals, it's challenging to know what you're working towards. Break down your goals into smaller, achievable steps, and set deadlines for each step.

2. Find an Accountability Partner

Having an accountability partner can help you stay on track. This can be a friend, family member, or a mentor. Someone who understands your goals and is willing to hold you accountable can be a great motivator.

3. Track Your Progress

Tracking your progress is essential in staying accountable. Keep a record of your achievements and setbacks, and reflect on them regularly. This will help you stay motivated and focused on your goals.

4. Celebrate Your Wins

Celebrating your wins, no matter how small, is vital in staying motivated. Take the time to acknowledge your accomplishments, and reward yourself for your hard work.

5. Be Honest with Yourself

Honesty is the key to accountability. Be honest with yourself about your progress and setbacks. Admit when you've fallen short, and take the necessary steps to get back on track.

In conclusion, staying accountable is an essential element in achieving success. By setting clear goals, finding an accountability partner, tracking your progress, celebrating your wins, and being honest with yourself, you can stay motivated and focused on your goals. Remember, accountability starts with you. Take ownership of your actions, and you'll be on your way to achieving your dreams.

04

Chapter 4: Overcoming Obstacles

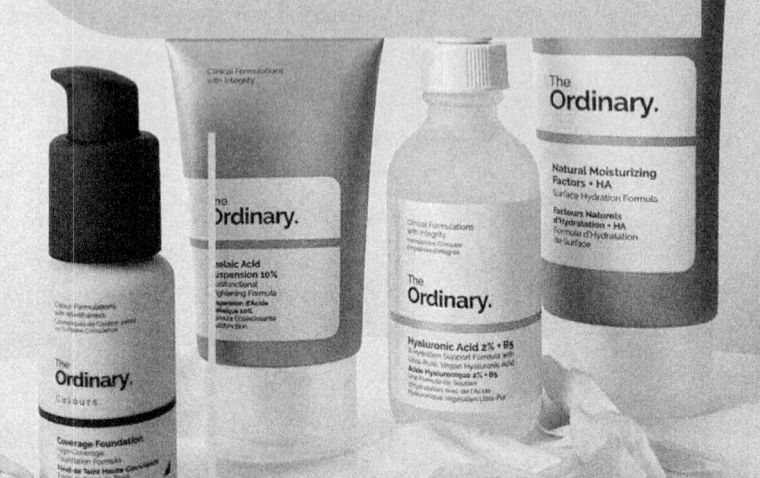

Find Your Spark: Motivational Encouragement for Women

Dealing with Fear and Failure

and "self-help".

Fear and failure are two of the most common obstacles that keep us from pursuing our dreams and achieving our goals. They can be paralyzing, causing us to doubt ourselves and our abilities. But the truth is, fear and failure are not to be feared, but rather embraced as opportunities for growth and learning.

When it comes to dealing with fear, it's important to understand that fear is a natural response to the unknown. It is our body's way of protecting us from potential harm. However, when fear becomes excessive, it can hold us back from taking necessary risks and making progress in our lives.

One way to overcome fear is to face it head-on. This means stepping out of our comfort zones and taking action despite our fears. It also means reframing our mindset around fear, understanding that failure is not the end of the world, but rather a stepping stone towards success.

Speaking of failure, it's important to understand that failure is not the opposite of success, but rather a necessary part of the journey towards success. It is through failure that we learn, grow, and improve.
It is through failure that we become resilient and develop the skills necessary to overcome obstacles.

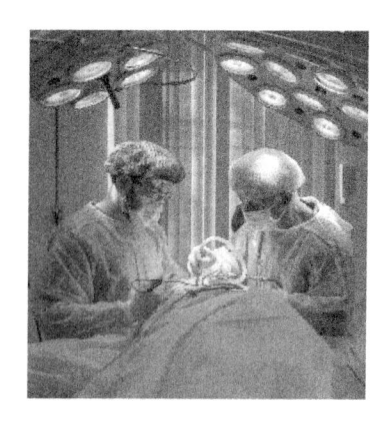

When faced with failure, it's important to avoid self-blame and instead focus on the lessons learned. This means reframing our mindset around failure and understanding that it is not a reflection of our worth or abilities, but rather an opportunity to learn and grow.

In conclusion, fear and failure are two common obstacles that can hold us back from achieving our goals and pursuing our dreams. However, by embracing them as opportunities for growth and learning, we can overcome our fears and use failure as a stepping stone towards success. Remember, you are capable of achieving anything you set your mind to, so don't let fear or failure hold you back. Embrace the journey and trust in your abilities.

Staying Positive During Difficult Times

and "self-help."

Life can be tough, and we all face difficult times. It's easy to get bogged down by the challenges we face, and it's natural to feel overwhelmed and negative. However, it's important to remember that we have the power to choose how we react to these difficult circumstances. We can choose to let them get us down, or we can choose to stay positive and keep moving forward.

Staying positive during difficult times is not always easy, but it's essential. When we stay positive, we are better able to cope with the challenges we face, and we are more likely to find solutions to our problems. Here are some tips to help you stay positive during difficult times:

1. Focus on the positive: It's easy to get caught up in negative thoughts and feelings when we're going through a tough time. However, it's important to focus on the positive aspects of our lives. Make a list of everything you're grateful for, and remind yourself of these things every day.

2. Connect with others: It's important to have a support system during difficult times. Reach out to friends and family, and don't be afraid to ask for help. Connecting with others can help us feel less alone and can provide us with the support we need to get through tough times.

3. Take care of yourself: It's essential to take care of ourselves during difficult times. This means eating healthy, getting enough sleep, and taking time for ourselves. Self-care is not selfish, and it's essential for our well-being.

4. Stay focused on your goals: When we're going through a tough time, it's easy to lose sight of our goals. However, it's important to stay focused on what we want to achieve. Keep taking small steps towards your goals, and remember that every step counts.

5. Keep a positive attitude: Finally, it's essential to keep a positive attitude. This means focusing on the good things in our lives, and not dwelling on the negative. It's not always easy, but with practice, a positive attitude can become a habit.

In conclusion, staying positive during difficult times is not always easy, but it's essential for our well-being. By focusing on the positive, connecting with others, taking care of ourselves, staying focused on our goals, and keeping a positive attitude, we can get through even the toughest of times. Remember, we have the power to choose how we react to difficult circumstances, and we can choose to stay positive and keep moving forward.

Finding Support and Encourage ment

As women, we often carry the weight of the world on our shoulders. We are expected to be the caretakers, the nurturers, the breadwinners, the homemakers, and so much more. It's no wonder that sometimes we can feel overwhelmed and alone.

But it doesn't have to be that way. Finding support and encouragement can make all the difference in our lives. Here are some tips on how to do just that:

1. Surround Yourself with Positive People

The people we surround ourselves with can have a huge impact on our lives. Seek out friends and family members who are positive, supportive, and uplifting. These are the people who will cheer you on when you're feeling down and celebrate your successes with you.

2. Join a Support Group

Whether it's a group for moms, entrepreneurs, or people with similar interests, joining a support group can be a great way to connect with others who understand what you're going through. You'll gain new perspectives, receive valuable advice, and make new friends along the way.

3. Find a Mentor

Having a mentor can be a game-changer in your life. A mentor can offer guidance, support, and encouragement as you navigate your personal and professional life. Look for someone who has achieved what you want to achieve and reach out to them for advice.

4. Seek Professional Help

Sometimes we need more than just a friendly ear. If you're struggling with mental health or other personal issues, don't hesitate to seek professional help. A therapist or counselor can provide you with the tools and support you need to overcome your challenges.

Remember, finding support and encouragement is not a sign of weakness. It's a sign of strength. By surrounding yourself with positive people, joining a support group, finding a mentor, or seeking professional help, you'll be better equipped to tackle life's challenges and find your spark.

Find Your Spark: Motivational Encouragement for Women

05

Chapter 5: Creating a Positive Mindset

Find Your Spark: Motivational Encouragement for Women

Developing a Growth Mindset

and "self-help".

Developing a Growth Mindset

One of the most important things that you can do in life is to develop a growth mindset. This is the idea that you can learn and grow from your experiences, failures, and challenges. By embracing a growth mindset, you can overcome obstacles, achieve your goals, and become your best self.

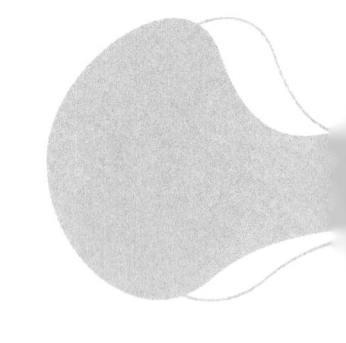

The first step in developing a growth mindset is to understand that your abilities and intelligence are not fixed. Instead, they can be developed and improved over time. This means that you can learn new skills, improve your performance, and overcome obstacles with the right mindset and attitude.

To cultivate a growth mindset, it's important to adopt a positive attitude towards challenges and failures. Instead of giving up or feeling discouraged, you should see these experiences as opportunities to learn and grow. By embracing a "growth mindset," you can improve your resilience, take risks, and achieve your goals.

Another key element of a growth mindset is the belief in your own potential. This means that you should have confidence in your abilities to learn and grow, even when faced with obstacles and setbacks. By believing in yourself and your potential, you can overcome self-doubt and achieve your dreams.

To develop a growth mindset, it's also important to embrace the power of "yet." This means that you should recognize that you may not have achieved your goals or mastered a skill yet, but with practice and persistence, you can achieve anything you set your mind to.

Finally, cultivating a growth mindset requires a commitment to lifelong learning and personal growth. This means that you should always be seeking new knowledge, skills, and experiences, and be open to feedback and constructive criticism.

In conclusion, developing a growth mindset is essential for achieving personal and professional success, overcoming obstacles, and becoming your best self. By adopting a growth mindset, you can cultivate resilience, confidence, and a lifelong love of learning and personal growth. So, embrace the power of "yet," believe in your own potential, and commit to lifelong learning and personal growth, and you can achieve anything you set your mind to!

Practicing Gratitude

Practicing Gratitude Gratitude is a powerful tool that can provide numerous benefits to our lives. It is the act of being thankful for what we have instead of focusing on what we lack. When we cultivate gratitude, we develop a positive mental attitude that leads to greater happiness, improved relationships, and a more fulfilling life.

To practice gratitude, we need to shift our focus from what we don't have to what we do have. This can be as simple as listing three things we are grateful for each day. It can be anything from the roof over our heads to the food we eat or the people we love. By acknowledging what we have, we cultivate an attitude of abundance that attracts more positivity into our lives.

Another way to practice gratitude is to reflect on the challenges we have faced and the lessons we have learned. Instead of dwelling on the negative aspects of a situation, we can focus on the positive outcomes and growth we have experienced. This helps us to see the silver lining in even the toughest situations and appreciate the resilience we have developed.

Gratitude also helps us to cultivate stronger relationships. When we express gratitude towards others, we acknowledge the value they bring to our lives. This strengthens our bond with them and increases the likelihood of them reciprocating the gratitude. It also helps us to develop empathy and understanding towards others, which is essential for healthy relationships.

Finally, gratitude helps us to find our spark. When we focus on what we have instead of what we lack, we develop a positive outlook on life that fuels our motivation and ambition. It helps us to see the potential in ourselves and the opportunities around us. This can lead to greater success, fulfillment, and a sense of purpose.

So, let us practice gratitude each day and experience the transformative power it can bring to our lives. Let us be thankful for what we have, appreciate the lessons we have learned, and express gratitude towards those around us. By doing so, we can find our spark and live a life that is truly fulfilling.

Cultivating Self-Compassion

and "self-improvement".

Self-compassion is a powerful tool that can help you overcome self-doubt and negative self-talk. It is the act of treating yourself with kindness and understanding, just as you would treat a friend or loved one. Cultivating self-compassion requires practice, but it is a skill that can be learned and strengthened over time.

To begin cultivating self-compassion, start by recognizing and acknowledging your negative self-talk. Pay attention to the thoughts that go through your mind when you make a mistake or face a challenge. Are you harsh and critical of yourself? Do you beat yourself up over small mistakes? Once you are aware of these negative thoughts, challenge them. Ask yourself if you would say the same things to a friend in the same situation. If not, try to reframe your thoughts in a more positive and compassionate way.

Another important aspect of cultivating self-compassion is learning to forgive yourself. We all make mistakes and have moments of weakness. It is important to acknowledge these moments, but also to forgive ourselves and move on. Holding onto guilt and shame only adds to our stress and anxiety.

Practicing self-care is another important aspect of self-compassion. Taking care of your physical and emotional needs can help you feel more confident and capable. Make time for activities that bring you joy and relaxation, such as exercise, reading, or spending time with loved ones.

Finally, remember that self-compassion is not selfish. In fact, it is essential for building strong relationships and being a supportive friend and partner. When we treat ourselves with kindness and compassion, we are better able to extend that same love and understanding to others.

In conclusion, cultivating self-compassion is a key component of self-improvement and motivation. By learning to treat ourselves with kindness and understanding, we can overcome self-doubt and negative self-talk, and build stronger, more fulfilling relationships with ourselves and others. Remember to be patient with yourself, and practice self-compassion every day.

06

Chapter 6: Taking Action

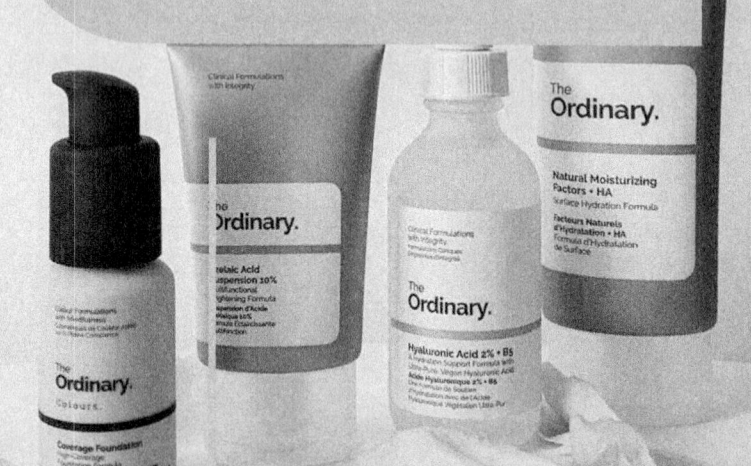

Find Your Spark: Motivational Encouragement for Women

Breaking Down Your Goals into Actionable Steps

and "self-improvement". As women, we often have a lot on our plates. Whether it's work, family, or personal goals, it can be overwhelming to try and tackle everything at once. That's why it's important to break down your goals into actionable steps - small, achievable tasks that will help you move closer to your ultimate objective.

The first step in breaking down your goals is to clearly define what it is you want to accomplish. This could be anything from starting a new business to running a marathon to learning a new language. Whatever it is, make sure it's specific, measurable, and attainable.

Once you've defined your goal, it's time to start breaking it down into smaller steps. Start by brainstorming all the different tasks that need to be completed in order to achieve your goal. Then, organize these tasks into a logical sequence, so that each step builds on the one before it.

For example, if your goal is to run a marathon, your actionable steps might include things like:
- Research and choose a training plan
- Buy proper running shoes and gear
- Start with shorter runs and gradually increase distance
- Incorporate strength training and stretching into your routine
- Register for the race and set a date to work towards

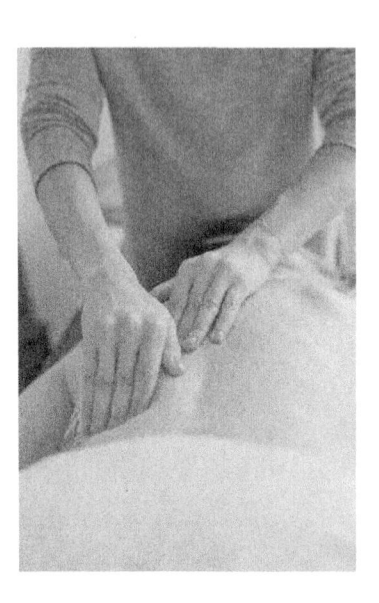

Breaking down your goals into actionable steps not only makes them more manageable, but it also helps to keep you motivated. Each time you complete one of your smaller tasks, you'll feel a sense of accomplishment and progress towards your ultimate goal.

Remember, it's okay to adjust your plan as you go along. Life is unpredictable, and sometimes unexpected obstacles will arise. But by breaking down your goals into smaller steps, you'll be better equipped to handle any challenges that come your way.

So, whether you're trying to start a new business, improve your health, or learn a new skill, take the time to break down your goals into actionable steps. With a clear plan in place, you'll be well on your way to achieving your dreams.

Overcoming Procrastination

and "self-improvement".

Overcoming Procrastination

Procrastination is a habit that is all too easy to fall into. It's easy to put off doing something until tomorrow, or next week, or next month. But the problem with procrastination is that it robs us of our time and energy, and prevents us from achieving our goals and dreams.

If you're struggling with procrastination, there are a few things you can do to overcome it and get back on track.

1. Identify the root cause

The first step in overcoming procrastination is to identify the root cause of why you're putting off a task. Are you afraid of failure? Are you overwhelmed by the size of the task? Are you simply bored or disinterested? Once you identify the reason behind your procrastination, you can start to develop a plan to overcome it.

2. Break it down

One of the most effective ways to overcome procrastination is to break a big task down into smaller, more manageable pieces. This can help you to feel less overwhelmed and give you a sense of progress as you work through each piece.

3. Set deadlines

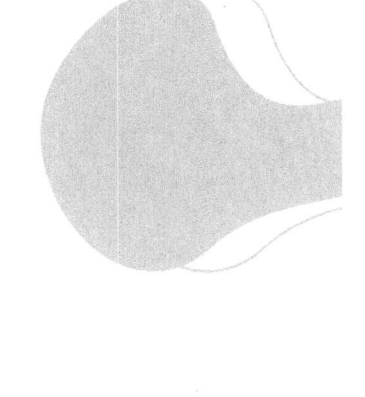

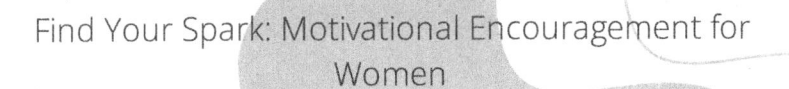

Deadlines can be a powerful motivator to get things done. Set a realistic deadline for yourself and commit to it. If you're struggling to meet your deadline, consider enlisting the help of a friend or accountability partner to keep you on track.

4. Eliminate distractions

Distractions are a major contributor to procrastination. Identify the distractions in your life that are keeping you from getting things done, and eliminate them. This might mean turning off your phone, closing your email, or finding a quiet space to work.

5. Celebrate small victories

Finally, it's important to celebrate the small victories along the way. When you complete a task, take a moment to acknowledge your accomplishment and reward yourself in some way. This can help to keep you motivated and focused on your goals.

In conclusion, procrastination is a habit that can be overcome with the right mindset and strategies. By identifying the root cause, breaking tasks down, setting deadlines, eliminating distractions, and celebrating small victories, you can overcome procrastination and achieve your goals and dreams.

Celebrating Your Accomplishments

and "self-help."
Celebrating Your
Accomplishments
Women often have a hard time recognizing their accomplishments. We are wired to focus on our flaws and shortcomings, thinking that our successes are just a stroke of luck. But it's time to change that mindset. Celebrating your accomplishments is an essential step towards feeling motivated and empowered.

First, you need to acknowledge your achievements. Write them down, no matter how small they may seem. Did you finish a task on time? Did you get a promotion at work? Did you finally find the courage to start a new project? These are all successes that deserve recognition.

Next, take the time to celebrate your accomplishments. Treat yourself to something that you enjoy, whether it's a fancy dinner, a spa day, or a new outfit. Celebrating your successes shows that you value yourself and your efforts.

It's also essential to share your accomplishments with others. Let your friends and family know about your successes, and don't be afraid to ask for their support and encouragement. Celebrating your accomplishments with others can be a great motivator and can help you stay on track towards achieving your goals.

Find Your Spark: Motivational Encouragement for Women

Finally, don't forget to reflect on your accomplishments. Take the time to think about what you learned from your successes, and how you can apply that knowledge to future challenges. Reflecting on your accomplishments can help you build confidence and resilience, which are essential traits for achieving your goals.

In conclusion, celebrating your accomplishments is a critical step towards feeling motivated and empowered. It's time to recognize your successes, celebrate them, share them with others, and reflect on what you learned. By doing so, you will build the confidence and resilience needed to achieve your goals and find your spark.

Find Your Spark: Motivational Encouragement for Women

Find Your Spark: Motivational Encouragement for Women

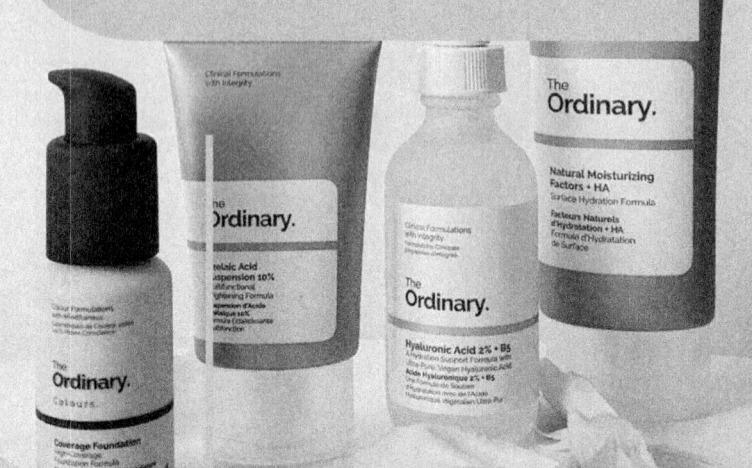

07

Chapter 7: Maintaining Your Motivation

Find Your Spark: Motivational Encouragement for Women

Developing a Routine

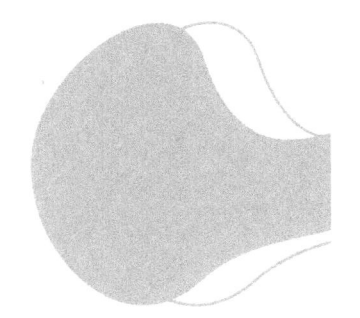

and "self-improvement".

Developing a Routine

Developing a routine is a key element in achieving success, no matter what your goals may be. When you have a routine, you create a sense of structure and order in your life. This will help you to stay organized and focused on what you want to achieve.

Creating a routine can be challenging at first, but with practice, it will become second nature. Here are some tips to help you get started:

1. Start small: Don't try to overhaul your entire life all at once. Start with small changes, like waking up 15 minutes earlier or taking a 10-minute walk after lunch.

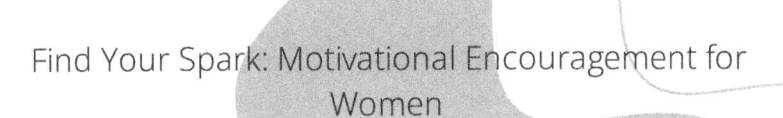

2. Set goals: Write down your goals and break them down into smaller, achievable steps. This will help you stay motivated and track your progress.

3. Be consistent: Stick to your routine as much as possible. Consistency is key when it comes to building habits.

4. Make it enjoyable: Your routine should be something you enjoy doing. If you dread it, you're less likely to stick with it.

5. Be flexible: Life happens, and sometimes your routine may need to be adjusted. Don't beat yourself up if you miss a day or have to change things around.

6. Celebrate your progress: Take time to celebrate your achievements, no matter how small they may seem. This will help you stay motivated and continue to strive towards your goals.

Remember, developing a routine takes time and effort, but the rewards are worth it. By creating structure and order in your life, you'll be able to achieve your goals and become the best version of yourself.

Staying Inspired

and "self-improvement".

Staying Inspired

Every woman wants to live a life full of inspiration and motivation. However, we all know that life can be tough, and our daily routine can be overwhelming. We often get caught up in the monotony of our daily tasks, and our inspiration and motivation can take a hit. But what if I told you that you can stay inspired, even in the toughest of times? Here are some tips that can help you stay inspired and motivated, no matter what life throws at you.

1. Find Your Why

The first step towards staying inspired is to find your why. Your why is your purpose, your reason for doing what you do. It's the thing that gets you out of bed in the morning and keeps you going when the going gets tough. When you know your why, you can stay focused on your goals and stay inspired even when things get tough.

2. Surround Yourself with Positive People

The people you surround yourself with can have a huge impact on your inspiration and motivation. If you surround yourself with negative people who bring you down, it's going to be hard to stay inspired. On the other hand, if you surround yourself with positive people who encourage and uplift you, it's much easier to stay inspired and motivated.

3. Take Breaks

It's important to take breaks and give yourself time to recharge. Whether it's taking a walk outside, reading a book, or simply taking a nap, taking breaks can help you stay inspired and motivated. When you give yourself time to rest, you can come back to your work with renewed energy and inspiration.

4. Set Realistic Goals
Setting realistic goals is key to staying inspired and motivated. When you set goals that are too lofty or unrealistic, it's easy to get discouraged and lose motivation. However, when you set realistic goals that are achievable, it's much easier to stay inspired and motivated.

In conclusion, staying inspired is all about finding your why, surrounding yourself with positive people, taking breaks, and setting realistic goals. By implementing these tips, you can stay inspired and motivated, no matter what life throws at you. Remember, inspiration and motivation come from within, so always stay true to yourself and your purpose.

Overcoming Burnout

and "self-improvement."
Overcoming Burnout

Burnout is a real problem that affects many women today. It's that feeling of being exhausted, overwhelmed, and drained that can lead to negative emotions, decreased productivity, and even physical health problems. Burnout can be caused by various factors, including work-related stress, personal issues, and lack of self-care.

If you're experiencing burnout, don't worry, you're not alone. There are ways to overcome burnout and find your spark again. Here are some tips:

1. Recognize the signs of burnout

The first step to overcoming burnout is to recognize that you're experiencing it. Some signs of burnout include feeling tired all the time, lacking motivation, being irritable, and feeling disconnected from others. If you're experiencing any of these symptoms, it's time to take action.

2. Take a break

One of the best ways to overcome burnout is to take a break. This could mean taking a vacation, taking a day off work, or simply taking a few hours to do something you enjoy. It's important to give yourself time to rest and recharge.

3. Practice self-care

Self-care is essential for overcoming burnout. This could mean taking care of your physical health, such as eating well, getting enough sleep, and exercising regularly. It could also mean taking care of your mental health, such as practicing mindfulness, journaling, or seeking therapy.

4. Set boundaries

Setting boundaries is important for preventing burnout. This could mean saying no to extra commitments, delegating tasks, or setting limits on your work hours. It's important to prioritize your own well-being and not overextend yourself.

5. Find support

Finally, finding support is essential for overcoming burnout. This could mean confiding in a friend or family member, seeking support from a therapist or counselor, or joining a support group. It's important to know that you're not alone and that there are people who can help you through this difficult time.

In conclusion, burnout is a common problem that affects many women. However, by recognizing the signs of burnout, taking a break, practicing self-care, setting boundaries, and finding support, you can overcome burnout and find your spark again. Remember, taking care of yourself is essential for your well-being and happiness.

08

Chapter 8: Conclusion

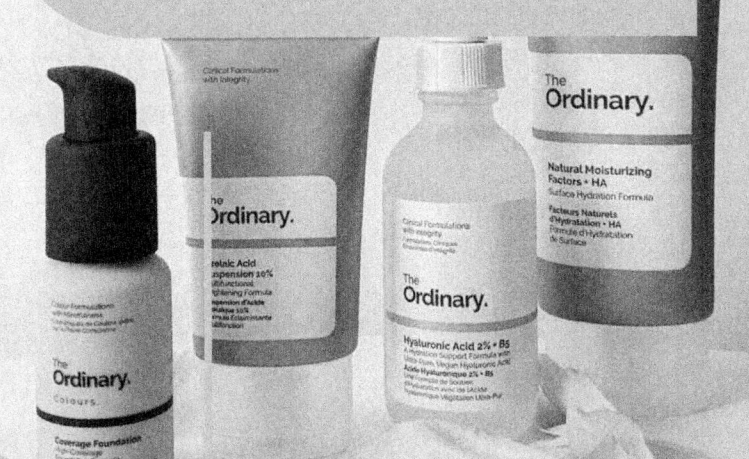

Find Your Spark: Motivational Encouragement for Women

Recap of Key Points

and "self-help".
Recap of Key Points
Throughout this book, we have explored various ways in which women can find their spark and stay motivated. Here's a recap of the key points discussed:

1. Self-awareness: The first step towards finding your spark is understanding yourself. Take time to reflect on your values, strengths, and areas of improvement. This will help you identify what truly motivates you.

2. Goal setting: Set clear and achievable goals for yourself. Break down your long-term goals into smaller milestones to make them more manageable.

3. Self-care: Taking care of yourself is crucial for staying motivated. Practice self-care activities such as exercise, meditation, and spending time with loved ones.

4. Positive mindset: A positive mindset is essential for overcoming challenges and staying motivated. Practice gratitude and positive self-talk to cultivate a positive mindset.

5. Embrace failure: Failure is a part of the journey towards success. Embrace your failures as opportunities to learn and grow.

6. Support system: Surround yourself with a supportive network of friends, family, and mentors. They will provide you with the encouragement and motivation you need to keep going.

7. Take action: Finally, take action towards your goals. Consistent action is the key to achieving success and staying motivated.

Remember, finding your spark is a journey, not a destination. Keep exploring, learning, and growing, and you'll find that your motivation and passion will continue to flourish.

Encouragement for the Journey Ahead

and "self-improvement".

Encouragement for the Journey Ahead

As women, we often find ourselves in a constant state of self-improvement. We want to be better mothers, better daughters, better partners, better employees, and better friends. We set goals, make plans, and work hard to achieve them. However, the journey towards self-improvement is not always easy. There are obstacles, setbacks, and moments of self-doubt along the way. That's why it's important to find encouragement for the journey ahead.

One of the best ways to find encouragement is by surrounding yourself with positive people. The people you spend your time with can have a huge impact on your mindset and your motivation. If you surround yourself with people who support and encourage you, you will be more likely to stay motivated and focused on your goals. Seek out friends, mentors, and colleagues who inspire you and lift you up.

Another way to find encouragement is by focusing on your progress, not your perfection. It's easy to get caught up in our mistakes and failures, but it's important to remember that progress is progress, no matter how small. Celebrate your successes, even if they seem small, and use them as motivation to keep going.

It's also important to take care of yourself along the way. Self-care is not selfish; it's necessary for your well-being. Make time for activities that bring you joy, whether it's reading a book, taking a bubble bath, or going for a walk. When you take care of yourself, you'll have more energy and motivation to pursue your goals.

Finally, remember that setbacks and failures are a natural part of the journey. Don't let them discourage you or make you give up. Instead, use them as opportunities to learn and grow. Ask yourself what you can do differently next time, and keep moving forward.

In conclusion, the journey towards self-improvement is not always easy, but it's worth it. Surround yourself with positive people, focus on your progress, take care of yourself, and don't let setbacks discourage you. With determination and encouragement, you can achieve your goals and find your spark.

Final Thoughts

and "self-help".
Final Thoughts

As you come to the end of this book, we hope that you are feeling inspired and motivated to find your spark and ignite your passion. Remember, your journey is unique and personal to you. Take the time to reflect on what truly brings you joy and purpose.
It's important to remember that setbacks and challenges are inevitable, but it's how we choose to respond to them that makes all the difference. Use these moments as opportunities for growth and self-discovery. Don't let fear of failure or rejection hold you back from pursuing your dreams.

Surround yourself with positive influences and a supportive community. Seek out mentors and role models who can guide and inspire you along the way. Remember that you are never alone on this journey.

Self-care is crucial to maintaining a healthy and balanced life. Make sure to prioritize your physical, emotional, and mental health. Take time to rest, recharge, and nourish your body and mind.

Don't be afraid to take risks and step outside of your comfort zone. Embrace new experiences and challenges with an open mind and a willingness to learn. Trust in yourself and your abilities, and don't let self-doubt hold you back.

Finally, remember that finding your spark is not a one-time event, but a continuous journey. Embrace the ups and downs, and enjoy the ride. Your spark may evolve and change over time, but as long as you remain true to yourself and your passions, you will continue to shine bright.

Find Your Spark: Motivational Encouragement for Women

I hope that this book has provided you with the motivation and encouragement you need to find your spark and live a fulfilling life. Remember, you are capable of achieving anything you set your mind to. Believe in yourself, and never give up on your dreams.

Find Your Spark: Motivational Encouragement for Women

Daniela has pursued a diverse range of professional development opportunities, including teaching, leadership and management training, first aid, event planning, food hygiene education, and yoga instructor (to name a few). This commitment to ongoing learning is a testament to her dedication to personal growth and the drive to serve as inspiration to help others progress. Masters in Education and aiming for freedom, smiling, loving her children while she spends more time with them and reaching her goal in impacting others. Her other skills include a keen enthusiasm for maintaining a healthy balance in her life, spending time with her family outside, travelling, boosting happiness and spreading love, sharing her heritage, and encouraging everyone to take little efforts towards being a better version of themselves.

Printed in Great Britain
by Amazon

50887330R00056